teach me about

Bathtime

Copyright © Joy Berry, 2022
Originally Published, 1986

All rights are reserved.

No part of this book can be duplicated or used without the prior written permission of the copyright owner, except for the use of brief quotations from the book.

For inquiries or permission requests contact the publisher.

Published by Joy Berry Enterprises
www.joyberryenterprises.com

teach me about

By JOY BERRY

Illustrated by Bartholomew

I get my toys before my bath begins.

I do not choose toys that could get ruined in the water.

I choose my bath toys carefully.

I do not want to get my clothes wet.

I take my clothes off.

I do not want to get burned

or feel cold.

I test the water with my hand

to see if it is too hot

or too cold.

I need help when I take a bath.

I make sure

that a big person is around

before I get into the water.

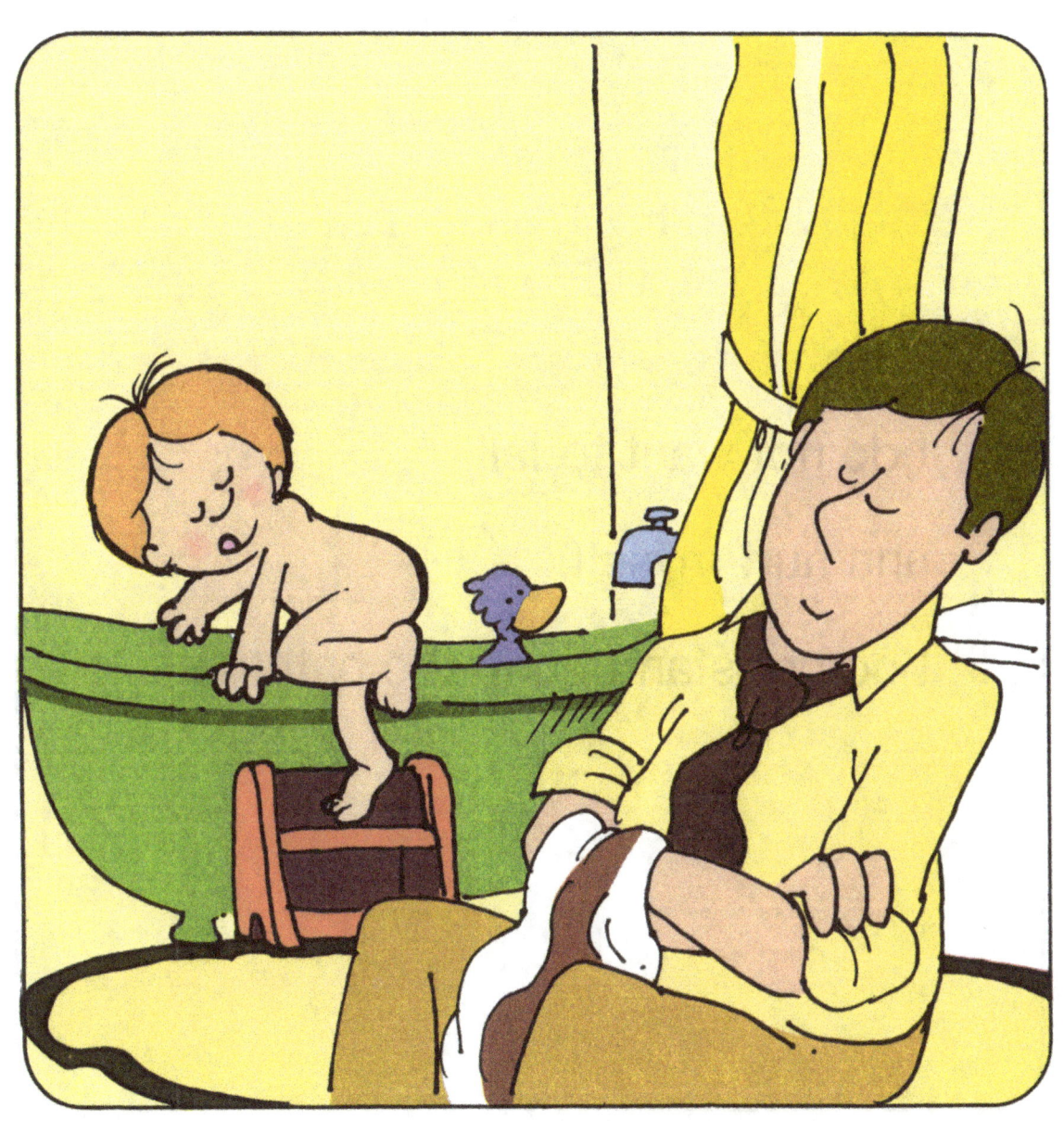

I do not want to fall

and hurt myself.

I do not stand up in the bathtub.

I do not want to ruin my bath toys.

I play with them very carefully.

I do not want to splash water outside of the tub.

I do not splash or play too roughly.

I want to get my body clean.

Mommy or Daddy washes me with soap.

I help.

We are careful

not to get the soap

in my eyes or mouth.

I want to get my hair clean.

Mommy or Daddy washes my hair.

I help by sitting very still.

I do not want to get shampoo

in my eyes or mouth.

I close my eyes.

I close my mouth.

I do not want to slip and fall.

I get out of the water

slowly and carefully.

I do not want to stay wet.

Mommy or Daddy dries me.

I help by standing still.

My bath is over.

I am clean.

I smell good.

I feel good.

I am ready to get dressed.

helpful hints for parents about
Bathtime

Dear Parents:
The purpose of this book is
  to tell children why they need to take a bath, and
  to show them how to make bathtime safe as well as fun.
You can best implement the purpose of this book by
  reading it to your child, and
  reading the following *Helpful Hints* and using them whenever applicable.

BATHTIME PREPARATION

Bathtime will be easier for everyone if you are prepared. You might want to have some of these items on hand:
- mild soap
- baby shampoo
- washcloth
- miscellaneous toys
- towel
- cotton swabs
- clothes to be worn

These things can be stored on a shelf or in a drawer near the tub.

Preparation for bathtime may also include doing these things:
- Take the phone off the hook so that you will not be disturbed.
- Hang a "do not disturb" sign on the front door so that people will not interrupt you.
- Heat the bathroom if it is cold so your child will not be uncomfortable.

BATHTIME SAFETY

Make a bathtime safe by following these rules:
- Sponge-bathe your infant until the umbilical cord falls off.
- Bathe your infant in the kitchen sink. Not having to stoop or kneel will make it easier and therefore safer for you to bathe your baby.

- Use an infant tub or a vinyl, open-weave basket in the bathtub to confine your child to a smaller, safer area.
- Use a bath mat or nonslip stickers on the bottom of the bathtub. If these are not available, put a terry-cloth towel in the bottom of the tub to prevent your child from slipping.
- Test the temperature of the bath by putting your elbow into the water. If necessary, adjust the temperature of the water so that your child will not be accidentally burned.
- Place a wet hand towel or washcloth on the faucet to soften bumps and help your child avoid possible burns.
- Never leave a child under six years of age unattended in the bathtub. This is to avoid an accidental drowning or injury that can occur in and around the tub.

BATHTIME COMFORT

Keep shampoo out of your child's eyes by following one or more of these procedures:
- Have your child hold a washcloth over his/her eyes.
- Allow your child to wear swim goggles.
- Put petroleum jelly on your child's eyebrows and lids.
- Cut the crown out of a shower cap and have your child wear it.

Keep water out of your child's nose and ears by using one or more of these items:
- Nose plugs that can be purchased at a sporting goods store.
- Custom-made ear plugs that can be obtained from your ear, nose, and throat doctor.
- Homemade ear plugs that can be made by placing cotton in

the ears and covering the cotton with Silly Putty. Silly Putty can be purchased at a toy store.

BATHTIME TOYS

Bathtime will be fun for your child if you provide toys that can be used in the bathtub. In addition to commercial toys, here are some other items that can be used:

- spray or squirt bottles
- plastic containers (with and without lids)
- wooden spoons
- strainers
- measuring cups and spoons
- dippers
- plastic tubing and straws
- balloons filled with water or air
- Ping-Pong balls
- rubber balls
- sponges
- eggbeaters
- wire wisks
- Styrofoam cups
- squirt guns
- a plastic bottle of bubble-blowing mix

A clear plastic container can be used as a water scope. Remove the lid. Push the container, bottom first, into the water. Keep the rim of the container above the water level. Do not allow water to flow into it. Look into the container for a clear, underwater view.

Here are some suggestions for using and storing bath toys:
- Rotate the toys each week by offering a few and storing the rest. This will prevent your child from becoming bored with any one item.
- After each bath, put the toys that have been used into a nylon net, drawstring bag or a plastic bucket with holes punched in the bottom. Rinse the toys in the container with clean water and hang them on the faucet to dry.

BATHTIME ACTIVITIES

Here are two recipes for bubbles and finger paints that can be used in the bathtub:

Bubble-blowing
- Mix together the following:
  1/4 cup liquid detergent
  1/4 cup water
  1 teaspoon sugar
  1 tablespoon glycerin
- Cut four short slits at one end of a straw. Dip this end into the solution. Blow on the other end of the straw to make bubbles.

Finger Paints
- Mix together the following:
  1/2 cup Ivory Snow soap flakes
  1 cup warm water
  1 drop of food coloring (optional)

Beat the mixture until it is the consistency of shaving cream. This finger paint can be used on the tub, the tile, or the body. Remind your child to use this mixture carefully as it will burn if it gets into the eyes.

Other activities might include:
- **Searching for sunken treasures.** Place objects on the bottom of the tub. Invite your child to find the objects. The clear plastic water scope may add to the fun.
- **Fishing.** Place floating objects, like Ping-Pong balls, into the water. Give your child a strainer to fish for the items.
- **Bathing the baby.** Give your child a doll that is suitable for the bathtub (one that can be immersed in water without being damaged). Let your child bathe the doll.
- **Cleaning the tub.** Give your child a clean rag, sponge, or scrubbing brush to clean the tub for fun.

BATHTIME FINALE

When bathtime is over, you can motivate your child to get out of the tub by doing one or more of the following:
- Use a timer to let your child know when bathtime is over.
- Offer to give your child a story or snack after bathtime.
- Invite your child out of the tub with a towel that has been warmed in the dryer. Someone other than the person giving the bath should warm the towel.
- Pull the plug if your child resists getting out of the tub. When the water is gone, your child will get cold and want bathtime to be over.

BATHTIME FOLLOW-UP

Here are some additional suggestions for cleaning and grooming your child:
- Begin proper dental care when the first tooth appears. Small toothbrushes can be purchased and used for baby teeth.
- Clip your child's fingernails and toenails right after bathtime while the nails are soft. It is easiest to trim the nails of uncooperative children while they are asleep.
- Cut your child's hair outdoors where the lighting is better and the cleanup is easier.

www.ingramcontent.com/pod-product-compliance
Lightning Source LLC
Chambersburg PA
CBHW081410070526
44583CB00020B/2753